# Video Game Heroes

# LINK:
## LEGEND OF ZELDA HERO

★ x1986

Kenny Abdo

Fly!
An Imprint of Abdo Zoom
abdobooks.com

**abdobooks.com**

Published by Abdo Zoom, a division of ABDO, P.O. Box 398166, Minneapolis, Minnesota 55439. Copyright © 2021 by Abdo Consulting Group, Inc. International copyrights reserved in all countries. No part of this book may be reproduced in any form without written permission from the publisher. Fly!™ is a trademark and logo of Abdo Zoom.

Printed in the United States of America, North Mankato, Minnesota.
052020
092020

Photo Credits: Alamy, AP Images, fandom, Flickr, Getty Images, Pond5, Shutterstock, ©Robotortoise p.cover / CC-BY-SA, ©BagoGames p.cover, 4, 6, 11, 15, 16 / CC BY 2.0, ©Ali Mohammed p.12, 14 / CC BY-SA 3.0, ©Farley Santos p.17 / CC BY-SA 2.0
Production Contributors: Kenny Abdo, Jennie Forsberg, Grace Hansen
Design Contributors: Dorothy Toth, Neil Klinepier

**Library of Congress Control Number: 2019956193**

**Publisher's Cataloging-in-Publication Data**

Names: Abdo, Kenny, author.
Title: Link: Legend of Zelda hero / by Kenny Abdo
Other title: Legend of Zelda hero
Description: Minneapolis, Minnesota : Abdo Zoom, 2021 | Series: Video game heroes | Includes online resources and index.
Identifiers: ISBN 9781098221454 (lib. bdg.) | ISBN 9781644944196 (pbk.) | ISBN 9781098222437 (ebook) | ISBN 9781098222925 (Read-to-Me ebook)
Subjects: LCSH: Video game characters--Juvenile literature. | Legend of Zelda (Game) --Juvenile literature. | Nintendo video games--Juvenile literature. | Heroes-Juvenile literature.
Classification: DDC 794.8--dc23

# TABLE OF CONTENTS

# LINK

Link may not say much, but his heroic actions speak much louder than words.

With his **iconic** green cap, longsword, and **spirit**, Link travels through Hyrule fighting for good.

# PLAYER PROFILE

Shigeru Miyamoto set out to make a game that reminded him of being an adventurous child. He wanted to recreate that same excitement for players.

Miyamoto felt Link should be
universally familiar to players.
Designer Takashi Tezuka looked at
Disney's *Peter Pan* for inspiration.

Miyamoto felt players should have to think in order to advance in the game. So, they packed *The Legend of Zelda* with puzzles, action, and places to explore.

# LEVEL UP

*The Legend of Zelda* was released in the United States in 1987. It sold out instantly. Link's quest to save Princess Zelda is considered the first of modern **role-playing (RPG)** video games.

*Zelda II: The Adventure of Link* quickly followed in 1988. *Zelda II* is the first video game to combine **RPG** and **platforming**. Some players found the game too difficult.

In the series there are different
**incarnations** of Link. However, all the
characters share the same **spirit** of
a legendary hero. Players must work
toward building up their hero status
throughout the game.

Link has stopped evil kings in *Ocarina of Time* on the Nintendo 64 **console** and retrieved the Master Sword in *Breath of the Wild* on the Switch.

Link has popped up in many other Nintendo series. He is a playable fighter in every *Super Smash Bros.* game. Link can even race in *Mario Kart 8.*

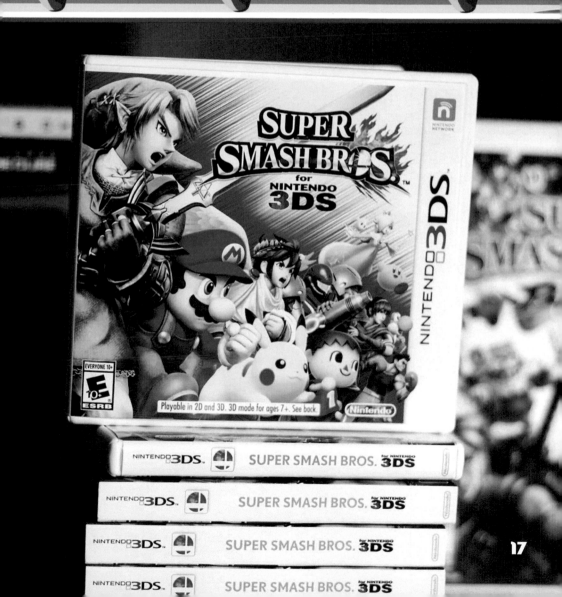

# EXPANSION PACK

VIRTUAL REALITY 3D HEADSET
+ BLUETOOTH® CONTROLLER

VIRTUAL REALITY 3D HEADSET
+ BLUETOOTH® CONTROLLER

Link has appeared in dozens of comic books. He even starred in his own cartoon, *The Legend of Zelda* in 1989.

The **iconic** song "Overworld Theme" is used in every *Zelda* game. It was written by Koju Kondo in just one day. Today, **symphonies** are dedicated to playing it around the world.

According to Metacritic, *Breath of the Wild* is the second-best reviewed game of the 2010s. Showing that Link is not just a hero to Princess Zelda, but to gamers around the world.

# GLOSSARY

**console** – a type of device that you play video games on.

**iconic** – commonly known for its excellence.

**incarnation** – a character regarded as embodying or exhibiting similar qualities or ideas to another.

**platformer** – a video game where players must control the character to jump and climb over platforms.

**role-playing game (RPG)** – a game where players take the roles of characters in the fictional world.

**spirit** – the way a character feels or thinks, as marked by qualities such as courage.

**symphony** – a concert orchestra.

# ONLINE RESOURCES

 **Booklinks**
## NONFICTION NETWORK
**FREE!** ONLINE NONFICTION RESOURCES

To learn more about Link, please visit abdobooklinks.com or scan this QR code. These links are routinely monitored and updated to provide the most current information available.

# INDEX